My Daily Du'as

"Call upon Me; I will answer you"　　*(Surah Ghafir 40:60)*

INTRODUCTION

All praise is for Allah. We praise Him, seek His aid and ask for His forgiveness. We seek Allah's refuge from the evils of ourselves and from our evil actions. Whomsoever Allah guides then none can misguide him, and whomsoever Allah misguides then none can guide him. I testify that none has the right to be worshipped but Allah alone, having no partners, and I testify that Muhammad is His slave and Messenger.

ACKNOWLEDGMENTS

Sheikh Ibrahim Shokra Abu Malik
Abu Khalil
H Irmal Abu Maimuna

When we wake up in the morning we say:

الْحَمْدُ لِلَّهِ الَّذِى أَحْيَانَا بَعْدَمَا أَمَاتَنَا وَ إِلَيْه النَّشُورُ

Praise be to Allah who gave us life after death and unto Him will be the return.

Al-hamdu lillahi-ladhi ahyana ba'dama amatana wa ilayhin-nushur.

(Al-Bukhari & Muslim)

When we enter the toilet we say:

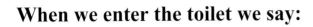

اللّهُمَّ إِنِّى أَعُوذُ بِكَ مِنَ الْخُبْثِ وَالْخَبَائِث

O Allah! I seek refuge in you from all evil and evil doers.

Allahumma inni a'udhu bika minal khubthi wal-khaba'ith.

When we leave the toilet we say:

غُفْرَانَكَ

I seek your forgiveness (O Allah).

Ghufranak.

(Al-Bukhari & Muslim)

4

After completing Wudu we say:

أَشْهَدُ أَنْ لا إِلهَ إِلّاَ اللهُ وَحْدَهُ لا شَرِيكَ لَهُ،

وَأَشْهَدُ أَنَّ مُحَمَّداً عَبْدُهُ وَرسُولُهُ، اللَّهُمَّ اجْعَلْنِي مِنَ

اَلْتَّوَّابِينَ، وَاجْعَلْنِي مِنَ الْمُتَطَهِّرِينَ

I bear witness that there is no deity but Allah. He is Alone. He has no partner. And I bear witness that Muhammad is His servant and Messenger. O Allah! Make me of those who are repentant and of those who purify themselves.

Ash-hadu an la illaha il-Allah wahdahu ia sharika lahu wa ash-hadu anna Muhammadan abduhu wa rasuluh. Allahumma j'alni min at-tawabin, wa j'alni min al-mutataharin.

(Muslim & At-Tirmidhi)

Before we pray we say:

اَللّهُمَّ بَاعِدْ بَيْنِي وَبَيْنَ خَطَايَايَ كَمَا بَاعَدْتَ بَيْنَ الْمَشْرِقِ
وَالْمَغْرِبِ، اَللّهُمَّ نَقِّنِي مِنْ خَطَايَايَ كَمَا يُنَقَّى الثَّوْبُ الْأَبْيَضُ مِنَ
الدَّنَسِ، اَللّهُمَّ اِغْسِلْنِي مِنْ خَطَايَايَ بِالْمَاءِ وَالثَّلْجِ وَالْبَرَدِ

O Allah! Separate me (far) from my sins as you have separated (far) the East and West. O Allah! Cleanse me of my sins as white cloth is cleansed from dirt. O Allah! Wash me of my sins with water, ice and snow.

Allahumma ba'id baini wa baina khataya-ya kama ba'adta baina al-mashriqi wal-maghrib.
Allahumma naqqani min khataya-ya kama yunaqqa aththawbul abyad min ad-danas.
Allahumma ighsilni min khataya-ya bil-ma'i wal-thalji wal-barad.

(Muslim)

8

Before we eat we say:

بِسْمِ اللّٰه

In the name of Allah.

Bismillah.

(Bukhari & Muslim)

After we have eaten we say:

الحَمْدُ لِلَّهِ الَذي أطعَمَني هذا وَرَزَقَنيه مِن
غير حولٍ مِنّي و لاقُوَّةِ

All praise be to Allah who has fed me this, provided me it with neither ability on my part nor strength.

Al-hamdu lillahi-ladhi at'amani hadha, wa razaqanihi min ghairi hawlim minni wa la quwwa.

(At-Tirmidhi)

When we get dressed we say:

بِسْمِ الله، الَحَمْدُ لِلَّهِ الَّذِي كَسَانِي هَذَا
الثَّوْب ورزَقنِيهِ مِنْ غَيْرِ حوْلٍ مِنّي ولاقُوَّةٍ

In the name of Allah, all praise is for Allah who has clothed me with this garment and provided it for me, with no power or might from myself.

Bismillah, Al-hamdu lillahi-ladhi kasani hadha ath-thawba wa razaqanihi min ghairi hawlim minni wa la quwwa.

(Abu Dawud & At-Tirmidhi)

15

Before we leave our house we say:

بِسْمِ اللهِ، تَوَكَّلْتُ عَلَى اللهِ، وَلاَحَوْلَ وَلاَ قُوَّةَ إِلاَّ بِاللهِ

In the name of Allah. I depend on Allah. There is no ability or power (for us) except by the leave of Allah.

Bismillahi tawakkaltu 'ala Allahi wa la hawla wa la quwwata illa billah.

(Abu Dawud & At-Tirmidhi)

16

When we enter our car (or any type of transport) we say:

الله أَكْبَر،الله أَكْبَر , الله أَكْبَر , سُبْحَانَ الَّذى سَخَّرَلَنَاهذا وَمَاكُنَّالَهُ مُقْرِنِينَ وَإِنَّاإِلَى رَبَّنَا لَمُنقَلِبُونَ

Glory to Him Who has subjected these to our (use), for we could never have accomplished this (by ourselves). And to our Lord, surely we will be returning.

Allahu Akbar, Allahu Akbar, Allahu Akbar,
Subhan al-ladhi sakh-khara lana hadha
wa ma kunna lahu muqrinin, wa inna ila Rabbina lamunqalibun.

(Qur'an 43:13-14 & Muslim)

When it is raining we say:

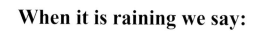

O Allah, may it be a beneficial rain cloud.

Allahumma sayyiban nafi'an.

(Al-Bukhari)

When it is windy we say:

اللَّهُمَّ إِنِّي أَسْأَلُك خيرَهَا وأَعُوْذُ بِكَ مِنْ شَرِّهَا

O Allah, I ask you for its goodness and I take refuge with you from its evil.

Allahumma inni as aluka khayraha, wa a'udhu bika min sharraha.

(Abu Dawud)

When we enter a mosque we say:

اللَّهُمَّ افْتَحْ لِي أَبْوَابَ رَحْمَتِكَ

O Allah, open for me the gates of Your mercy.

Allahumma iftah li abwaba rahmatika.

(Al-Bukhari & Muslim & Tirmidhi)

When we exit a mosque we say:

اللَّهُمَّ إنِّي أَسْأَلُكَ مِنْ فَضْلِكَ

O Allah, I ask You of Your benevolence.

Allahumma inni as aluka min fadlika.

(Al-Bukhari & Muslim)

When we enter our home we say:

بِسْمِ اللهِ وَلَجْنَا، وَ بِسْمِ اللهِ خَرَجْنَا، وَ عَلَى رَبِّنَا تَوَكَّلْنَا

In the name of Allah we enter and in the name of Allah we leave, and upon our Lord we place our trust.

Bismillahi wa lajna, wa bismillahi kharajna, wa 'ala Rabbina tawakkalna.

(Abu Dawud)

Before we go to sleep we say:

بِاسْمِكَ اللَّهُمَّ أَمُوتُ وَ أَحْيَا

In Your name O Allah, I live and die!

Bi ismika Allahumma amutu wa ahya.

(Al-Bukhari & Muslim)

Notes to Parents

1st Du'a   -   To be said **immediately** when you wake up in the morning.

2nd Du'a   -   To be said **before** you enter the toilet with your **left** foot.

3rd Du'a   -   To be said as you **exit** the toilet with your **right** foot.

4th Du'a   -   To be said **after** you have completed wudu.

5th Du'a   -   To be said **before** you pray. The Prophet (SAAS) used to say it before fard prayers.

6th Du'a   -   To be said **before** you eat.

7th Du'a   -   To be said **after** you have eaten and before you leave the place of eating.

8th Du'a   -   To be said **before** you get dressed.

9th Du'a   -   To be said **before** you leave your front door.